ACCIDENTAL WEATHER

SHEROD SANTOS holds a Ph.D. in English from the University of Utah, where he currently teaches. In 1978 Mr. Santos was awarded the Discovery/*The Nation* Award and a Utah Arts Council Award in Literature. His poems have appeared in numerous journals and magazines, including *The New Yorker, Poetry, The Nation, The Paris Review, Antaeus,* and *The Iowa Review*. Mr. Santos is the 1981 recipient of the Oscar Blumenthal Prize, given by *Poetry* magazine.

Accidental Weather

SHEROD SANTOS

Doubleday & Company, Inc.
Garden City, New York
1982

Library of Congress Cataloging in Publication Data
Santos, Sherod
  Accidental weather.
  I. Title.
PS3569.A57A65   811'.54   81-43594
ISBN 0-385-18050-0   AACR2
ISBN 0-385-18051-9 (pbk.)

ACKNOWLEDGMENTS

(A number of these poems originally appeared in slightly different versions.)

Antaeus: "The Garden-Party," "On the First Anniversary of Your Departure," "Sarah Coleridge at Greta Hall," "Self-Portrait" (as "Memory"), "Terra-Incognita," and "Winter Landscape with a Girl in Brown Shoes."
Black Warrior Review: "Sight-Seer" and "The Wait."
The Iowa Review: "Rain" (as "W.C.W.'s Moment of Suspense"). First appeared in *The Iowa Review.* Copyright © 1979 by The University of Iowa.
The Missouri Review: "Weather."
The Nation: "Lamentation" (as "Ancient Lamentation"). The Nation Magazine, Nation Associates, Inc.
The New Yorker: "Sirens in Bad Weather" and "The Art of Cruel Colors." Reprinted by Permission; © 1980, © 1981. The New Yorker Magazine, Inc.
The Paris Review: "Difficult Place." © Copyright 1979, *The Paris Review.*
Ploughshares: "The Beginning of Autumn." First published in *Ploughshares,* March 1982.
Poetry: "Begin, Distance" (April 1979), "Country Landscape" (April 1979), "Melancholy Divorcée (April 1979), "After a Long Illness" (October 1980), "On the Last Day of the World" (October 1980), "Three Fragments" (October 1980), "The Breakdown" (August 1981), "The Evening Light Along the Sound" (August 1981), "View from the Hotel Lobby" (August 1981), and "Waiting for the Storm" (August 1981). Reprinted by permission of the Editor of *Poetry.*
Quarterly West: "Burning the Fields." First published in *Quarterly West,* Fall/Winter 1981.
The Seattle Review: "Late November" and "A Visit Home."
The Sonora Review: "Angina." First published in the Fall of 1980. © Copyright 1980, *The Sonora Review.*
Western Humanities Review: "The Palace Hotel at 2 A.M." First published in *Western Humanities Review,* Winter 1980.

Six poems from section Three appeared in a limited edition volume: *"Begin, Distance"* (Greenhouse Review Press, 1981).

"Country Landscape" and "Childhood" were reprinted in the *Anthology of Magazine Verse and Yearbook of American Poetry* (Monitor Book Company, Inc., 1980 and 1981), editor, Alan F. Pater.

"Melancholy Divorcée" was reprinted in *Pushcart Prize V,* 1980–1981 edition, Pushcart Press, editor, Bill Henderson.

"Genesis" by Delmore Schwartz, © 1982 by Kenneth Schwartz. Reprinted by permission of New Directions Publishing Corporation. Unpublished poem.

for Lynne McMahon

THE NATIONAL POETRY SERIES

1982

Accidental Weather, by Sherod Santos
   (Selected by Charles Wright)

The Mud Actor, by Cyrus Cassells (Selected by Al Young)

Hugging the Jukebox, by Naomi Shihab Nye
   (Selected by Josephine Miles)

Second Sight, by Jonathan Aaron
   (Selected by Anthony Hecht)

The Incognito Lounge, by Denis Johnson
   (Selected by Mark Strand)

Contents

Three

Why a little curtain of flesh
on the bed of our desire?

—WILLIAM BLAKE

One

ON THE FIRST ANNIVERSARY
OF YOUR DEPARTURE

Somewhere along the back hills, the giant cranes
are calling again, low-flying along the black ravines
and lifting over the headlands
where the red-tipped aspen leaves are dipping
soundlessly, by the thousands,
                          into the ascending shade—
and beyond the hills, stretching for miles,

the gradual tides of grass withdraw from the stony fields.

At work, yesterday evening, I remembered,
and for the first time
it occurred to me, the weather's changing,
as it did then, so unexpectedly,
like a curtain yanked from a window,
                          and from now on,
from the soft hills, the cold
will be rising like a fine powder
into the broken branches, the thin air, and the clouds,
dark-edged and threatening along the horizon . . .

                          And then it was dark.
The lamp was on, the window black,
and my face was filling up the glass,
as strange to me as yours
had seemed that morning as you lay
on the bed, not sleeping, and said my name,

and waited. You did the right thing
after all,

      and so
last night, staring at the window,
I thought of you then, once,
and took a long time, but the face was still
too far away,

      as if flawed by a slow-falling snow.

ANGINA

On some nights moonlight
troubles the curtain-edges,
the wallpaper roses wind
up their stems, and stars
drift slowly out into
the open. And some nights
clouds shadow the park
across the way, and I
think of deer standing
a moment, all clumsiness,
but grandly, beside a pond,
and I wonder if it was I
who killed them, you
or I, or was it some other
thing, some feathery sigh
which, like an arrow,
riffles, without a sound,
through the living heart.

There is something rising
in my blood. From its perfect
center, each night, in sleep,
it begins, rising like a thin
shaft of sunlight through
the trees, until I awaken,
and the light is standing
through me, and the darkened
wallflowers drift heavenward

in sleep. But even then,
beyond that whiteness which
sifts down from the sky, beyond
the whiteness of everything
alive, and standing still
in an open place, something
waits, as if in tall grasses,
waits, and then comes forward
rising on the wind.

THE ART OF CRUEL COLORS

At the touch of a match, the neighbor's raked
pile of vari-colored leaves goes up effortlessly
in a draft of smoke . . . the hoar-frost sparks
across the marbled walk, along the scaling-ladder
vines which turn the red bricks black. Still,
the neighborhood holds its place, but the sky
has changed from saffron to a flamy pale-blue . . .
Can we say the eye offends less cruelly now
that the summer's blossoms are blown? Years ago,
my mother's old German gardener took an axe
to all her prize *tziganes* one quiet Sunday
in the middle of June, to hack out some memory
he'd found embedded in that blood-shot rose he'd
plotted all his life to breed . . . and all through
the evening those awful blossoms lay, still throbbing,
on the darkening lawn, as though the petals
themselves contained some color we too feared.

A VISIT HOME: *for my brother*

It's late, and I've been sitting up reading
in your room, Mary and the children sleeping,
the sparrows along the eaves sleeping.
And as I reach up now to turn off
the lamp, already the morning
isn't so far away, already that first glow

has smoked the river's glass. Today,
the river is low, and there's just enough wind
you can hear the box-elder spilling
its leaves onto the tool-shed
like rain—how many days began
just this way, with you and me rising in a pale

blue light, dressing, then crossing the field
with our gear, and down the bank to the rock-ledge,
only talking in whispers, when we did.
I walked there again last evening,
and the same river-murmur still
poured through the trees, through the canebrake

and weeds, until it seemed, for a moment,
I had never been away—and there was something
else that washed past me then, something dim
and alive that had moved through
our world the way the blind
carp moved beneath that shelf of stone,

far down below our silent stares, in some
deep place in the dark where we could not see
what we saw: and still, poised above that
nightblack water, we waited with
our backs against a tree
for that moment when, like the first glimmer

of dream, some glitter and silvery light
would rise breaking in the mind, breaking the water's
surface where we'd cast our lines out
beyond the edge of a riffle,
beyond the edge
of that world, where the closed world lay.

SQUALOR

The dwarf lime-trees tied to their stakes
must be digging through the underpinnings
of the porch. House paint bleeds across
the double panes—or have the garden flowers'
colors simply oozed out of the flowers?—
and not one swallow has risen unrejected
into the air. The massive green wilderness
has awakened among the tumuli of excavations
for its Aztec, sleeping gods—Quetzalcóatl
and Tláloc—who, like us, wish only to remain
in their rooms. Each year the season brings
us back for no other reason than to waste
our days sunning on the beaches, but instead,
like the scudding black clouds, we're only
staggered by the light now, now the sun.

VIOLENCE

Rainclouds have been stacking up
against the horizon for hours,
and I can't sleep. Wrapped
in the climbing ivy, the house still
shudders, and whenever the wind lifts
pineneedles slide in patches down
the pitched roof. It is the beginning
of autumn. Why else would so many
trees surround my sleep? Standing
at the window, I can barely see,
beyond that vast stretch
of pineforest, the glow from the lights
of the city, which is, even now,
something more than I expected.

Nothing has changed. I've been
in the country three months,
and still, each night, some new
distraction arrives, like a moment
of unexpected feeling: moonlight
just broke through the clouds
and fell into my room, onto a table
where a glass of violets dilates
the watery, white air. Maybe that
is why people are always so kind
to these hills. Maybe that is why
the landscape always seems to prefer us
this way: we should not be alone.

The summer's heat has blistered
the glacial stones along the valley
floor, but now the days
are cooling, and the redwings
are disappearing from the fields.
Now, in the evenings, I sit out
on the porch and watch the water
beetles closing in circles on
the weed-choked pond: there is nothing
to be afraid of. As soon as the sun
sets, the pond recedes into the distance
where the dairy barns and silos

are making their way in the dusk,
and it's as if I could turn my back
on all of this, as if there were
an end, even of feeling. But lying
in bed at night, and before
I know it, I am living again
in that memory of myself, in all those
moments, and each one a silence
that would be a pond, or a cloud, each one
rising up, mute and black, and shaded
over like dead leaves on dead.

THE BREAKDOWN

I

The sun scanned the river with its lidless
eye; before the heat had choked the saffron
fields, already the fishing-boats spotted
the calms, already our table was laid

for a homecoming. Mother's blue bedroom
window steamed behind the light-chinked blind: there,
awhile, her heart was still quiet enough,
a small boat bobbing on the horizon.

II

I dug in wet sedge for a woodchuck's hole:
the murky, rank, underwater smell when
I pulled my hands out with a sucking sound,
like a sob, and the imprints filled with mud.

There were puffy white clouds when she stepped out
from the shade. Or was it the heaviness
of the stock-still air that made the shadows
grow increasingly larger around her?

III

By evening the boats had crossed, without sail,
the glassy waters of the Sound. The gulls
intensified their treble calls—passing
masts were blunted now on the shallow sky.

On the other bank, the pulp-mill had just
shut down: water rats returned to the weeds
by the open sluices; a hip-booted
worker dragged his rake through the sawdust piles.

IV

She stood too long beside the riverbank.
The fronting fishermen's huts had gone blank
in the moonlight; and when the wind lifted
a few leaves fell, and the water's surface

shuddered, as if from emotion . . . Perhaps
she only grew more distant then, staring
downriver as if staring down a road
when there is nothing on it but the night.

V

The moon floated through the overhanging
willow, as if nosing through shoals; the bed-
spread swam with splotches of light, yellow-white
on pale-blue; and each wind-shift shook the tree

so the air would fill with those silvery
leaves, like scales scraped down the length of an eel.
I pulled the window-blind shut, but the hand
did not loosen, in the darkness, its grip.

AFTER A LONG ILLNESS

Now beneath the aspen trees moonlight blends
the lilac and ailanthus, and the seasonal
wild roses spill their cups along the pathway
stones . . . What can I say? In my mother's house
today, no one is dying. There is a bank
of swallows asleep in the eaves above her bedroom
window, and their sleeping makes a sound
like the movement of water, which is thinner than blood,
but which awakens still the sound of those footfalls
down the carpeted hallway toward her door.
Now above the aspen trees the clear stars drift
in the moonlight of the shining sky, as if on some
long sigh they were carried away, and today
there is no one dying in my mother's house.

SIRENS IN BAD WEATHER

The wet streets are undisturbed by that chronic
high whine—as of a fish hawk over the blue
glaze, over the refracted light which slips in
through the cloud-breaks. A week's rain has
pasted the elm leaves to the sidewalk, and stuck
some against the buildings, and to the tires
of a refrigerator truck which unloads nightly
in the alley below—it's like a brown mildew
spreading through the city. And the constant drip,
drip, in which the passersby in their rainhats
and galoshes seem submerged . . . like the man standing
in the intersection next to his crumpled car:
round-mouthed and motionless, as if underwater,
his scream still rising a block away.

SELF-PORTRAIT

There is a town outside Paris called Enghien-les-Bains
where, three years ago, in mid-March,
I stood waiting for a taxi to the casino.

I had gotten off the train in the suburbs.

Because the sun had just set, the backdrop to the town
was inflamed, and the shuttered windows
of the houses there seemed closed in a derisive manner.

There was no one on the station platform, although
tule fog moved back and forth across the boards
like a crowd of people that kept expecting
another crowd of people to arrive.

And off to the side of the platform,
a mattress that had been gutted
and tossed on top of a pile of debris
shone compulsively in the failing light . . .

An hour later, a tablecloth
was flung out over a table with a sudden *whump!*
—without looking in that direction,
I wondered: what difference could it possibly make?

And through the window I could see just the letters R-N-O

click on and off above the marquee.

Then a woman steps full-body into the doorway
and says: "So, there you are."

SIGHT-SEER

The evening's sluggish procession—
the fish stalls are closing up along
the quays, the fountains sift down
their watery light and heavy gulls

drift in sideways from the sea . . .
It's quiet here. Across the street
a local bride just drew back
the curtains in the hotel window,

her hair still flecked with bluets
and crocus petals. In the morning
she passed by in a veil; now,
the veil is folded in a hatbox.

And for the rest of the morning,
as though not to be outdone
by ceremony, the sun kept breaking
through the stormclouds, igniting

the rain-puddles and lifting a thin
blue rubble above the esplanade.
And beneath the streets I could hear
the sump-pumps still drawing

at the terminals: it was
as if someone were lying there
below me in the dark,
in a darkness which rose and fell

as with a doubled heart. Under
such an illusion, how could I help
but think I was never so
far apart from anything as now . . .

There were olive leaves strewn
along the wet streets, and now
and then the rustling of clothes.

CHILDHOOD

How it is I returned
to this one memory all
morning and through mid-
afternoon could not work,
confused still by what
had, or would not, come
back to me: a few small
drops of rain on my
Sunday shoes, the sun
plunged into the rose-gray
summit behind the woods,
and settling, overhead,
like waterbirds (you can't
tell how many, their wings
overlapping), the high yellow
clouds, and a voice, at
intervals, calling my name
across that farflung
sky—no, across the disced
back pasture where I
had wandered, not lost or
frightened, but as in a drift
of leaves—and so it was
I turned then and saw, not you,
but a winter moon rising
out of the suburbs like a pearl
earring lifted into place
by a hand, too long ago,

to be sure, to know what
it means, or the time
it takes, which was all
your life, Mother, and
all of mine.

Two

KAFKA

Dearest, tonight the stars are infinitesimal,
the avenue is lit by fern-shaped flames
blazing from a melting pot
on the corner, and the air is strewn
with the dank odor of the flower-vendor's
discarded, rotting flowers.
Nothing feels quite my own tonight.

Just now, as I sat here, the second hand
suddenly took my breath away, and for a moment
it seemed I had clocks all over my body,
as though I were wearing a costume
of clocks, and at intervals
one ticked off a minute here and there.
If only you weren't so far away.

Is anything more absurd than for you
to be travelling through the world?
Though you accuse me of sounding lighthearted,
for months my entire nervous system
has been in a state of constant turmoil—
I rarely sleep, erratic pulse, little blood.
Does that ease your mind?

A review of my work has finally appeared.
What do you think of this: "Kafka's bachelor art . . ."
Each day brings me closer to anonymity.
So you should not take too seriously this

dabbler in graphology you keep "bumping into."
Experience should tell you, I am
by no means "extremely sensual." Nor am I

"determined in my behavior." Even "artistic
interests" is not true, as anyone could see
by the way I address you in these letters.
Surely you understand by now,
my life is split in half, so to speak:
one side feeds on your life with bulging cheeks
and could be a great man, and happy.

The other is adrift, like a cobweb—
an entire day without headaches is all
it asks, though rarely receives. So why
cause me such anxiety? About the time
you were writing that letter, I must have been
sitting on a bench in the Dornersplatz—
was I drowsing?—the entire horizon was bruised

by stormclouds, and then, as if he had known me
for life, a man protected only by a thin
summer shirt kept walking back and forth
in front of me, staring—and when I asked
myself why, I could only imagine it was because,
like yourself, he was dressed for a different
climate . . . Please, no more reprisals!

And how you sadden me at times. With your
renewed enthusiasm for the Müller exercises?
Which you've always resisted? And even though
now you must wait until dark to perform them
with your blouse off, and the window open,
and so prevent the people opposite
from joining in the exercises with you!

Forgive me if I seem always complaining.
Recently I am caught defending myself
at every turn: just yesterday, at a restaurant,
a woman across from me, out of boredom,
fell from her chair. And I, from the same
affliction this evening, brushed my hair
in the mirror five times in succession.

But you are tiring of this. And now
I must go and put this in the mails, and so
prevent you, once more, from languishing
in those false feelings of relief
that I have stopped sending you letters.
Please allow me to send you a kiss
upon that wide soft brow with its beneficent

glow—and one piece of advice: when your cousin
starts to talk again in her sleep,
place a towel carefully over her face.
Finally, love, your letter contained
this one contemptuous remark, which, as such,
gave me great pleasure: "Surely
you'll be able to survive another 3 months."

I confirm this with my signature:

                                    Franz

RAIN

As he was walking past a mill shed on his way
home late in the day,
a wood-chip flew off an axe

and nicked him on the temple.

He nodded politely
to the man inside with the axe.

The sun rolled down.
The marsh dropped casually into place.

So little trembling.

Hardly had the shops closed that night,
and the townspeople begun to sort through their pockets,
than a wind came up

and bent down the grasses,

and he turned from his dresser to look outside
at the few leaves
blown darkly across.

"A splinter flew off an axe,"
he said to himself.

And when he went downstairs later that night
he found his wife had left out

a cup, with a packet of cocoa beside it.

And he was also surprised by the sound
of the rain starting up
which sounded to him like splinters,

thousands of splinters ticking the windows.

LAMENTATION

after the Nahuatl

My love is Azatlan, the vendor,
and each day as the small buds
fatten on the apple trees,
she grows thinner.
The fruit of this season will be bitter.

Before the new moon,
her family will gather baskets
of those wild yellow blossoms
called *Brighter Than Stars*
and spread them out
across her body
as though she were a rich empty field,

and for two days, slowly,
she will draw into herself
the suns of each petal
to make her journey easy
and full of light.
The fruit of this season will be bitter,
and the flowers colorless.

ON THE LAST DAY OF THE WORLD

As usual, the guard who worked
the night shift at the boardwalk

returned home tired to his bed.
The sky began to whiten:

a window opened, and pigeons
were playing in the waterfounts.

There were fishermen smoking
on the docks, and someone

was already swimming when the sun
finally rose, and a few

passersby paused to watch that
gradual expansion of light along

the shoreline—it was more
as if someone had tilted the sea

toward the sun. The bakery
shutters were thrown open early

on the promenade, and at first
signs of heat the elderly

gathered, sipping their ices,
in the water-colored shade

of the palmleaves. And then
the bathers, with their bright

suits and baskets, began
to come out from the striped

tents and take their places
in the sand. And close

their eyes against the sun.
And softly, as though not

to disturb the afternoon, softly,
a radio love-song drifted out

through the air . . . so that
the guard turned over, once,

in sleep, and the sea gulls
made blue rings in the sky.

What else was there then, but
the music, and the warm sand?

THE PALACE HOTEL AT 2 A.M.

After the rain stopped, a warm channel-wind spilled
over the balustrade. The wicker lawn furniture
trembled with raindrops, and the raindrops flickered,

like the lit-ends of cigarettes, in the acetylene light.
I was in no hurry. Already you were in bed, and I
had watched for hours, from the Hotel Bar, the great

black clouds, back-lit by the moon, drive across the out-
lying hills . . . And then, just then, the waiter dropped
some coins on a plate. But before I could reply, a voice

behind me was whispering the lights out in the smoked
glasses—and overhead, the tiny points of the Milky Way
steamed in the darkness like candle-drippings.

THE LETTER

"The morning sun through this first snow still
warms the kitchen floor and lifts up the leaves
in the potted window plants. The house
sparrows have not yet abandoned their eaves.
But now, all at once, we are separated.
Look: a blueblack fly tosses and tosses
against the pane as if to lose itself
into the flowering absence of all that white.
It's snowing here today. Gradually, the poplar
groves are sinking into the past, and tomorrow
the sparrows will pick among the stones and find
something here, and there, and then leave.
What help is it to know sleep comes slowly
to your bed—you won't come, anymore, to mine."

MELANCHOLY DIVORCÉE

If you find yourself burning only now for a clumsiness
you have always possessed, for the way your coat hangs
    askew
on your shoulders, and the methodical, unthinking
    manner
in which you cross and uncross your legs in public,
then you will lie down in your bed at night
like a white and spotted thing
lying down in the moonlight of an open field;

and if you desire something out-of-place to disappear
from your breakfast table,
and the polished spoons and buttons and clean saucers
to carry their secret lives no longer
into the proud metaphor at the center of your sorrow,
then you desire no more than the eucalyptus leaves
thrashing the air at the beginning of October;

and if you discover the words *cacophony* and *colloquy*
and *calumny* recurring obsessively in the crossword puzzles,
and yourself expecting the windows of your neighbor's
house to stay lit much later than they do, and when
    they do
you worry, then you are beginning to understand
and forgive the Hungarian woman next door
for burning leaves all day in a blowing drizzle;

and if you learn to stop hating the grocery clerk
for counting your change out loud,
for the tattooed name on his wrist and the ugly way
the bills fall apart in your hands,
then you will grow to love the company
of the blue and nameless flowers
that pepper the earth around the olive trees each spring;

and if looking out your window you see the blue shirts
of the workmen moving up Highland Street to begin their
        day,
and if you catch yourself falling as easily as they
into the smell of coffee and the empty dream of
        the afternoon,
then you will stop turning to Browning and Chopin
to explain how you feel, and you will speak
in the anger and conspiracy of your own dark eyes;

and if walking downtown one blazing afternoon it occurs
        to you
that people have always said too much, that you have
        gone there
to hear their voices, and to watch your own image floating
with theirs through department store windows, then you
        are learning
the luxury of the warm earth floating beneath your feet,
and of the black waters at the mouth of the Corbuscu
        River
voluptuously reclaiming their silted shores.

VIEW FROM THE HOTEL LOBBY

Bleary by noon, the whitewashed
storefronts soak in the summer light,
in smoke from the charcoal braziers
and dust off the avenue running
red in the sun—and barely moving,
the awning's shadow inches across
the sidewalk, as if leading a lover
away. The watery air far outstreams
the mushroom fountain suspiring
in the square. And all afternoon dust
motes drift in pale slats across
the polished tiles, until, at last,
the evening arrives, quiet and apart,
and momentarily in the mind
as a time in winter you only half
recall: the light now trembling,
as if from emotion, and the heat-mist
settling, almost like snow, onto
the empty courtyard, the ornamental
trees, the leafless flamboyants.

THE GARDEN-PARTY

Beside an open window in the upstairs room,
she stands in the shadow of a flowering quince,
talking a little to herself
as she combs her hair. And each time

a breeze blows through, those tiny blossoms
seem to drink in the blue
air around her, as though a long thirst
were declaring itself in the leaves.

And though there is no rain, there is a sadness
of rain, and a sad smell of autumn
rising from the fields,
rising like the twilight off the grass in the fields.

How could one say
what traces of her world the swallows trailed
behind them now? What
dream of *longueurs* glittered on the air?

And how could one say how quickly the mystery
would fall from things
when the cars pulled up on the macadam,
and people in costumes began to appear

on the green baize of her darkening lawn—
for how tired and colorless
they seem tonight, like those anonymous
characters who die off-stage

in the opening scenes of a play.
So closing her eyes, she turns, instead,
toward the slow chough of the evening train
and the coming into view of that furrow

of smoke suspended in skeins
above the pine woods: and there, a moment,
it seems she can feel her own
life coming closer now, the circling embers

drifting down like a shower of stars
through her hair . . . but there is someone
calling from the garden below, and those
unhappy people are still waiting in the grass.

THREE FRAGMENTS

1.

Orion is rising, and the air
is tearing the paradise ferns
to shreds . . . nightbirds flick
the lighthouse eye like
metal filings . . . Worse things
could happen, just
in the sense we are this
or that, the slightest
trembling of the leaves.
The world is never very
simple. But this morning
the windows seemed smaller,
and the horses
wore a blanket of ice across
their manes. This morning,
love, the local hemlock
did not call you back
from the bridge.

2.

October has come with a wind
full of sand, and tall
waves that heave against
the harbor-pilings. Salt
traces speckle the tree
trunks like a million tiny
places of light, and in one
you are dozing on a lawn chair
in the sun, in a backyard
in Nogales, and all around you
the morning's dew has just
turned to steam. There are no
hard feelings. While I
stood on the pier this evening,
a small fishing boat
sailed in loaded down
with ptomaine: the stench
reached up and enlarged
my heart, the wheeling gulls
were momentarily distracted.

3.

Perhaps it's not too late.
The choke-flowers are still
knotted in the hedgerows.
And this morning when I woke,
a southbound freighter
was lodged on the horizon:
the horizon was rose and gray,
and the spiralling smoke uncoiled
along it like a party
streamer . . . I must have been
thinking of you. There was
some work to do, and the tufts
of mist were burning off
the cowpond. This morning
I lay awake a long time before
I sat up in bed, but with
the sun so full on that white
ship, and those reluctant
blossoms, my patience
was already wearing thin.

BESIDE THE BLUE RIVER

on the drowning of a childhood friend

The window gives on the black park benches
that encircle the shade trees hung with colored
bulbs . . . on a stretch of broken promenade
lit by tar pots escalading the river—
the room seems adrift in a perpetual dawn,
as though the world outside had only lightened
in the mind. And late at night the streets grow
quiet enough you can hear, inside your head,
insects throbbing at the screens—and the sound
is like the sound of a killing thing, some
shudder in the blood that rises to the brain,
the way the water hyacinths night and day
floating up from the south, seed themselves
along the waterways, and never will let go.

SARAH COLERIDGE AT GRETA HALL

The children have been down for hours, the fire dead,
and I cannot sleep. A cold wind has been sucking
at the edges of the house for weeks now,
and I'm as unaccustomed to this smell of wood-rot
and mulch, the darkening thickets and rank gullies,
as I am to the streak that petrified down my side
this morning when I came across, outside the butcher's,
a huge sow freshly gutted in the open air.
It may take years. This is our middle ground.

The moonlight nods to me through the taffeta curtains.
Beyond the hills, night-fishing boats push off the shoals
onto Blue Anchor Bay, row, and then draw in their oars,
    like geese
their wings, and wait. We live in these gradual spans
    of time,
pointless hours, the dark sky filling up and emptying out
    again,
and the days accumulate like leaves off the shaking trees.
The down quilt serves me its pool of blue light
—I am motionless beneath it, like the underside of a buoy,
moored to some dull conviction, some interim.

What loads me down discourages my brown-eyed
    children.
They rarely play. So much drifting of my thoughts
these days, I catch myself standing stiff from them,
and a chill creeps over me like the green-mold crabbing up
the bedroom wall. I am not young any longer. Is it

my own will kept me here since the day he left?
I'm beginning to think in different terms:
in my prayers I no longer even ask for happiness.
We get so little we deserve.

The minister cautions me I'm losing patience,
there is something to be gained from this, glorious
our pains. I must be disciplined. Each night
before bed I read the letters over by the fire,
the beautiful letters, more something to him, perhaps,
than me; or I tell the children stories about Bristol,
or the cottage at Clevedon; and it is worse.
Winter's close. The youngest has been coughing for
        a week,
and a feeling of death bores into me I can't withdraw.

It has been so long since last word came that it's become
difficult to even gauge the passing of the days.
Just this afternoon I encountered a young woman crossing
Parrett Bridge, trailing her hand slowly along the railing
like someone dragging the river for a body.
And when I looked away, the stars were out, moonlight
had fallen around me like a violet snow, and I was
surprised by my husband's presence walking beside me.
And I could not understand him in my widow's heart.

Three

WINTER LANDSCAPE WITH
A GIRL IN BROWN SHOES

to have snow: the fundamental situation
—DELMORE SCHWARTZ

The bridge was frozen. The river glared momentarily
like an arc-lamp
through the woods, the woods were silent.
Two huge black dogs lugged
an invisible rope up the hill
where the sun was coming to a quiet end,
and everyone who slipped and fell in the street
that day, fell the way a leaf falls
onto the hood of a car—
reluctantly, and with enormous contempt—
and was part of a true story.

She was little consolation in her brown shoes.
There were so many things the light averted
she could barely keep the sky
in place—which was now a hemisphere—
and she could not identify
any feeling she had that wasn't love.
Love: because the horizon had never appeared
so much like a shore, because snow
was just beginning to occupy the landscape
which was sinking,
inexplicably, like an unending page,
like too many waterfalls.

Then, too, the disarming wreaths gathered
around the streetlamps
did, in some way, apply to her. In the same way
that I am doing here. And eventually
the great shadow of the woods
fell across the upland pastures like a scarf—
if she had seen it—the blue scarf
that came loose from her throat
that morning and fell
across the white field of her pillow.

The most beautiful moments are beyond our reach.
And nothing is more ordinary
than a girl in brown shoes
walking down the street as it begins
to snow. Or love,
which comes mysteriously back to us.
And yet, as is always the case, it was
just so—and it asks the question
of what happened before all this time
we've been waiting, and drawn in so close
around ourselves, and at every moment
turning further in with an enthusiasm
we have rarely known in the past.

TERRA-INCOGNITA

Out of the morning dark, the pale self-generating
light of the asphodel moons against
the oriel casement, the green-stained brick—
and then that papery sound starts up again
in the maple trees. A month-long fog still hangs
from the leaves, as thick as smoke from torches
dipped in pitch . . . so thick our current
worries don't divide us anymore. By evening,
the air grows heavier still—we hardly notice
a sadness now has entered it, hardly notice
some other love has taken hold—as though
we'd drifted into one of those blank spaces
on ancient maps, that terra-incognita
cartographers once called "strange beauties."

BURNING THE FIELDS

It's three weeks to autumn, and ash
is drifting through the nearby hills—
ash and a sunset blaze rising off
the grass around the poplar trees,
which are rising, too, like smoke
and light, but rising,
all the same, with that pang of desire
which today has turned you away
from the fields: as if, while walking
this morning down the levee road,
it occurred to you the sky was darkening
for a reason now, a reason much more
than the grass on fire, but like
something in the heart, a star,
for example, rising like a spark
through the kindling air. But now
the wind has carried the fields
this way, in this sense we speak of,
seeing ourselves at the center
of things, even our illusions: like
looking out a window and finding there
the same face that years ago,
climbing a fence at dawn, awakened
the dogs barking across that flood
of burn in the sky . . . It's the way
we believe the world contains
some larger image of ourselves,
as though the burning meant

to explain, somehow, the way it feels
to *feel* this way, to distinguish
one moment from another until
all that remains is a little word,
like "love" or "pain," settling
on the air around us. And look,
today, how the smoke conceals
so many details that could mean
the same, how the sunlight
gutters in the topmost leaves, how
your reflection remains though you
have turned from the glass. And
consider, as well, how all this time
I've been sitting inside writing long
letters in which I scarcely even
mention such things—or that flush
of blood that rose in your cheek,
it goes without saying, like
a distant conflagration in the trees.

COUNTRY LANDSCAPE

for Carol Muske

This involves more than just the water standing
in that open field like an extended gasp,
or the one cloud drifting
toward a horizon you would never have imagined

so black—did I say *red* cloud?—or the newly-felled
tree's split membrane pulsing in the summerlight.
And it's not just the crops in a row like seasons,
either, that are responsible for this attitude,

although, paradoxically, that's what I've put down.
Sometimes I think it's the difficult matter of the heart.
Sometimes it could be almost anything except
what I've mentioned. All those things I decided against.

Perennial beauty. The dream of moss. And so much
silence wasted on us. This is the best place for it.
At least one mile is the distance between
the waiting weather and where you stand, at any moment.

And the question you'd be asking yourself here
is of the possibility for a better life, for greater desire,
though that is obscure, and the feeling of taking part.
The sad gulf that opens in the blood, like the weather.

Later, the moon and stars would rise
like boats diverging on a bay—
even then you wouldn't know what it means.
Unlike the stars, you would lose your breath,

you could hear your heart skipping stones,
and the memory of someone who once said:
"Your affections are seditious."
There are always sounds here. And small birds

that are learning to become chords—
as if the immense wind were not enough relief
extolling in the leaves which so often surround us.
Between you and me is an empty gesture,

I only recently understood that. And that gesture
has me sitting here confused by this piece of paper
which doesn't take into account the difficulty
of a street, a street repeatedly unconcerned with questions

of faith, or men on the move. I don't know what to say—
there are so many personal moments effaced in this light.
It's like this: dead insects blow across the floor.
They have never forgotten.

WAITING FOR THE STORM

The morning sun struck, like flint, the banked
clouds along the horizon—the cypress fumed
like smoking grass, tiny whitecaps ignited
beyond the estuary . . . and still the same
sighing of buoy and shorebird, the same tide
turning the deadwood away. When we pushed off
the dock, the bird-lime blazed bright white
on the pilings . . . but moments later the sun
was gone, and the sea surface touched by wind
began to quaver and toss like a wheatfield
catching fire. So what were we doing, what
were we thinking when we drew the oars in
and let our metal boat spin in that August harbor?

DIFFICULT PLACE

Sometimes in the evening I see
coming toward me, from a distance,
a kind of blossom: huge, blue, nodding
against this flat continent, taking
the fields away, and changing
irreversibly as the leaves
go by into that visible surface,
the dark, which takes me up,
again, still ill-at-ease among
the lamplight of this year's
perpetual turn. As if my
saying so made any difference,
this is, I assume you know, still
too close to you. Which doesn't
matter. And yet, if it were
anything else, like an elliptical
conversation, or a question of a loon
lifting off an empty tree,
or the room simply gathering
shadows in its usual fashion
and dispersing the dull light
—it would have meant the same.
Until you could almost hear
me say it: this is the room
where I live. That same
weakness. And before I sleep,
as always, I raise myself up
on one elbow and pour water

into a glass, and a dozen acacias
are bleeding on the pond again,
which I can see from the window,
the pond that so often thinks
of itself in human terms on nights
like these, or as a fire
around which sullen, disgruntled men
have gathered now that even
the moon has come out and confessed:
but I want to love you with both my hands.
Now that the landscape, like an
unwritten page, is occupied with so many
other details of pain—like the smoke,
coiling there so gracelessly,
the black smoke no one will talk about.

THE BEGINNING OF AUTUMN

The day has barely lifted before
the rain begins, and I sit down
at the desk littered with unanswered
letters and look out into the garden
abandoned now to ragweed and sour-
grass. The gentians we planted
have been dead for weeks, but still
their stalks turn strangely green,
and the spent leaves, too, scattered
on the ground around them: it is
the illusion of water and light,
of light playing on water, playing
in the mind, until the mind becomes
part of the illusion. A few hours
ago, waking in the dark, I could see
beyond the window these same clouds,
heavy and back-lit by the moon,
coming up from the south, and all
I could think was I could not hold
them back, could not keep them out
of our lives. But look, instead,
what a quiet now is settling
on the world: at the other end
of the house, Lynne is still sleeping,
the fir trees are murmuring above
their pitted roots, the dry earth
softening to shadow. And it seems
that hours from now, though everything

else might have changed again, this
same slow rain will still be filling
the air with that warm and ineffable,
that uselessly inturning light.

WEATHER

I am tired of filling up pages with words.
So, too, the weather's mood has awakened along
the pale branches. The mud ducks squatted
in the reeds behind my house are an abstract notion
of all that is bored in myself—there is no reason
to contradict them, or pretend I can change them
into something else: it is the point of view
of these ducks, their dull color, their particular
demands to be specific. The way a laborer holding
a shovel full of dirt is specific when he calls out
to a woman walking past without spilling the dirt
or disturbing the web of dust across his forehead.
But I keep thinking about the huge onyx
burning your soft hand, which is just an image,
and also obscene. Which is why you occur here
so often, anonymously, like a season occurring
to a grove of trees. That is what is meant
when I say I'm not prepared for what's going on
outside. Take this evening for example:
there is something called October
standing on the front porch, kicking its boots.
It is tired of doing its work, tired of complaining.

BEGIN, DISTANCE

The morning stars are a torment,
if you thought long enough, and yet
how much more unsettling is the reason
you have gone to the window in the first place.
Look what they do to the landscape.
You can see them standing in that certain detail,
like a sun–lit field full of children
learning to dance. Each one shining just so.
Or like a set of distinctions
impossible to take in. So that the sky
expands outward, and each time
you almost lose yourself, thinking of water,
in all directions.

Up to a point you can only imagine them,
because the eye plays past
its own hysteria, which is the same thing
as saying to yourself: *but think of the risk.*
And we expect to live out these moments
to their end, to the point
of greatest intensity, except the fields are.
And the trees still arrive there before us
constructing, out of fragments, the way
it would feel: what tipped the weeds
that way beside the pond–edge, why
is that shadow shaped like a glove,
who stunned the cattle into motion . . .

Only this time it's impossible,
so completely have I given up the idea
of the mountain's isolation,
and my own, which is like applause beneath
those stars. And there is a woman
who resembles this landscape
though it never occurred to me until now,
her deepening meadow, the burdens of space,
or how I might say we finally met, stranded
in the grass, the last green thing in Iowa.
Still, what bothers me more
is the sudden concussion of the snowline
where the semblance is unnatural, and asking
please—which makes me love it more—

and where, you'll say, no wonder the birds
flew away, and so on, assuming it's that
other condition, the one I can never conceal,
the one you call *wilderness,* though it might be
anything. We're in no danger. That much is like
a plane of sunlight shimmering on the horizon.
It's just the possibility we're giving in
—I don't know how—to some exquisite emotion.
As if none of this really happened at all,
down to the last negligible star, or the low
sun shifting the fields, or the woman
receding into the trees—and why wasn't she
more fully realized so close to the window?

THE EVENING LIGHT ALONG THE SOUND

I

As if the sky could no longer hold its color,
that pale blue light sifts down onto the water
like talcum onto a tabletop, or like the fine powder
of memory settling again in the mind in that hour
toward sleep, in that season toward autumn
when the trees begin to fill with a sorrowing air.
Still, there's a moment then when it all seems
so impersonal: no sign that something difficult
is reappearing in our lives, no image
of a feeling, but a feeling itself, like a mis-
directed letter from someone sad and faraway.

II

And it doesn't matter that in that quiet hour
you forget yourself awhile, that the sky
becomes a kind of mirror in which the face
grows dim, then disappears, like a coin
receding underwater. Even the early arrival
of the moon on the horizon only magnifies
the light's desire to turn all things
to light: how quickly it absorbs the sea-
birds drowsing on the air, although, tonight,
the evening star, like a bread-crumb dropped
on the water, is enough to bring them back again.

III

And the night is usually carried in on a breeze,
so that each time the water ripples the light
will darken, as if sprinkled with ash, and become
more fully a part of the air. But the truth is,
the light is sinking into itself, as we, in an absence
of light, will sink back into ourselves—
and it isn't a question, then, of how we feel,
but of how we hold ourselves out to the dark
when the dark closes down around us, and when,
momentarily, what light there is only glitters
in the mind, like a cluster of stars on the Sound.

LATE NOVEMBER

All day pinecones drop like shot birds
off the tree limbs, the tea kettle sings
from the iron stove . . . from under the leaf-mold,
winter's stain spreads like kerosene.
The cattle stop to watch us on our sunset walks,
ice-glitter sputtering in the pine-tops
and gullies, the house windows flaming just once
and going out. Our eyes have begun
to deceive us now, as if the heart can't
stand the strain of the earth, as if the ice age
had begun its heave and the longnecks
arcing overhead each evening were calling
back some other season, calling back
to us, and that dying fire in the trees.

THE WAIT

Tonight there is no one
on guard in the snow, above
the fields of our blood,
beside the collapsing jasmine
bushes. But what of the face
that continually refuses
the ice-flowers scrawled across
the windowpane, the moonlight
that continually refuses
the face? We can no longer
assume there is some chance
of passing unnoticed into
that quiet air. Or that *here,*
as where we are now, as
a rent in that air already
dissolving, is anything more
than the gathering tension
of the air itself.

There will be nothing
private in this, although
at one time it seemed
it would be just so: as if
only she could hear the music
drifting through the trees,
among the lights in the valley
far below. But now, each
moment that privacy becomes

a little less, a little more
unapproachable: it is a question
of a dozen stars named after
lakes, and on this particular
night she imagines their
cold waters lapping at
the edges of her sleeves.

Yes, and yet there is a kind
of contentment one feels
here too, as if we had never
left that place in which
we are yet to live: that place
which begins with a sigh
and ends in this slow turn
about the room surrounded
by an air of indifference.
But even in passing, her rose
complexion contains our desire
to understand, to lie down
in that circle of light—as if,
giving up the dream, she
could simply gaze beyond our
sorrows, and so draw them in,
the way the dawn light will tap
softly on the glittering hills,
just once, and the morning
stars move inland.